PHYSICS OF
SKATEBOARDING

PHYSICS OF SKATEBOARDING

Fun, Fellowship, and Following

Deji Badiru *and* Tunji Badiru

PHYSICS OF SKATEBOARDING
FUN, FELLOWSHIP, AND FOLLOWING

Author Credits: Deji Badiru

iUniverse books may be ordered through booksellers or by contacting:

iUniverse
1663 Liberty Drive
Bloomington, IN 47403
www.iuniverse.com
844-349-9409

ISBN: 978-1-6632-1751-6 (sc)
ISBN: 978-1-6632-1752-3 (e)

Library of Congress Control Number: 2021901685

Print information available on the last page.

iUniverse rev. date: 01/29/2021

DEDICATION

To the memory of Omolade Bisola, the
bud that has remained a bud

ACKNOWLEDGMENTS

Thanks to mom for helping to type some of the mathematical equations and the Appendix. The preparation of this book was a family team sport!

We also thank the readers and followers of ABICS Publications, who continue to provide inspirations and ideas for fun guidebooks for home, work, and leisure.

================================

ABICS Publications
Books for home, work, and leisure

ABICSurus Reader

A Division of AB International Consulting Services
================================

About ABICS Publications

Books in the ABICS Publications book series, published by iUniverse, Inc., on recreational, educational, motivational, and personal development books, include the titles below:

- Physics of Skateboarding: Fun, Fellowship, and Following
- My Everlasting Education at Saint Finbarr's College: Academics, Discipline, and Sports
- Secret of the 25th Hour in the Day: Getting More Done Each Day
- Kitchen Project Management: The Art and Science of an Organized Kitchen
- Wives of the Same School: Tributes and Straight Talk
- The Rooster and the Hen: Story of Love at Last Look
- The Story of Saint Finbarr's College: Contributions to Education and Sports Development in Nigeria
- Physics of Soccer II: Science and Strategies for a Better Game
- Kitchen Dynamics: The rice way
- Consumer Economics: The value of dollars and sense for money management
- Youth Soccer Training Slides: A Math and Science Approach
- My Little Blue Book of Project Management
- 8 by 3 Paradigm for Time Management
- Badiru's Equation of Student Success: Intelligence, Common Sense, and Self-discipline
- Isi Cookbook: Collection of Easy Nigerian Recipes
- Blessings of a Father: Education contributions of Father Slattery at Saint Finbarr's College

- Physics in the Nigerian Kitchen: The Science, the Art, and the Recipes
- The Physics of Soccer: Using Math and Science to Improve Your Game
- Getting things done through project management

ABOUT THE AUTHORS

Deji Badiru is a professor of industrial and systems engineering at the Air Force Institute of Technology (AFIT) in Dayton, Ohio. He is a prolific author of not only technical books, but also guidebooks for home, work, and leisure. His passion is writing about everyday events, observations, and social responsibility. He has won several awards for his teaching, research, scholarship, and administrative accomplishments.

Tunji (TJ) Badiru is a mechanical engineer at GENERGY Manufacturing, LLC in Moraine, Ohio. He received his BS degree in mechanical engineering from Wright State University, Dayton, Ohio. His recreational passions include skateboarding, soccer, and music. The cover image of this book is from one of his early skateboarding outings.

CHAPTER 1

INTRODUCTION TO THE JOY AND FUN OF PHYSICS IN SKATEBOARDING

The journey of writing this book traced back to the previous ABICS Publications books with the theme of "physics of" an object of interest. We have seen "the physics of soccer" and "physics in the kitchen." Beyond writing this book as a sports-oriented book, we also designed it as a motivational tool of educational introduction to STEM (Science, Technology, Engineering, and Mathematics).

This book is not intended as our goal or expertise to teach physics. Our goal is to provide sufficient motivational curiosity for readers to dig deeper into other sources of knowledge for the topics presented, primarily from a fun relational perspective, in the book. We particularly like the **Fun, Fellowship, and Following (F³)** overtone embodied in the subtitle of the book. The selected bibliography at the end of this chapter suggests some relevant books for further reading by the inspired readers.

Unlike team-based ball sports, such as like soccer, basketball, baseball, etc., where a human opponent is an impediment to a player's goals (pun intended) and even teammates could be a

1

hindrance, gravity is the primary opponent in skateboarding. "Soaring with Forces" could have been another appropriate subtitle for this book.

© Canstock photo: csp7958613/Snap2Art

Behind the Physics

Physics, as a science, is an essential part of human existence, whether in education, sports, industry, commerce, the home, and social settings. Physics is all around us and we should leverage it to have a better understanding of what we see, do, and experience. In fact, a caption in the website of the Physics of Soccer, www.physicsofsoccer.com, extols physics in the following statement:

"Biology determines what we are, Chemistry explains what makes us what we are, and Physics describes what we do." - Deji Badiru, Author of **The Physics of Soccer: Using Math and Science to Improve Your Game**, 2010

Physics explains the past, the present, and the future. Physics is the science of matter, energy, and the interactions between the two. Physics of skateboarding is addressed as a topic in this book both literally and figuratively. The literal part relates to the science and computational aspects of skateboarding. The figurative part presents "physics" informally as the process of accomplishing movements and actions in skateboarding. The approach of this book helps skateboarding enthusiasts to better appreciate the various aspects of the pursuit of skateboarding. In this case, cerebral pursuit is coupled with the physicality of the sport. This reminds us of the brain and brawn behind an endeavor. John Farnworth, the world-famous soccer-ball freestyle juggler is recognized for his skills in "bending the laws of physics." In 2018, he climbed 19,685 feet (6,000 meters) up Mount Everest in Nepal, while keeping a soccer ball in the air. That accomplishment demonstrated bending the laws of physics and defying the power of gravity.

The description of this book's title as "the physics of skateboarding" conveys the role of physics as a scientific tool to explain skateboarding motions. The metaphorical interpretation coveys the fact that the "physics" of something is often used to refer to how something is done; as in "how" to practice and execute movements in skateboarding and social interactions in skateboarding gatherings. For comparison, the book "**Factory Physics**" (1995) by Wallace Hopp and Mark L. Spearman presents fundamental "how-to" processes of manufacturing, including cycle time, throughput, quality, capacity, work-in-process, inventory, and reliability. The authors describe 22 laws (physics) for manufacturing that help managers better understand production, control cost, improve performance, and manage workers in a manufacturing plant. The Physics of Skateboarding seeks to accomplish a similar better understanding, control, performance improvement, and self-management in skateboarding groups. This leads us to explain the elements in the subtitles of the book: Fun, Fellowship, and Following.

Fun

Fun is the primary reason that individuals embrace skateboarding as a recreational pursuit. It is a fun activity that does not discriminate. Boys, girls, and adults all enjoy skateboarding, although at different levels of physical exertion. A visit to any organized skateboarding park quickly reveals how much fun people are having sailing, seemingly effortlessly, through the air in either geometrical patterns or in random directions. The fun aspect of skateboarding can be summed up in the following quote from the fun of soccer:

"I just want to get out there and play and have fun. After all, when I'm on a soccer field, that's when I'm at my happiest."

-Freddy Adu, professional soccer player

Along this type of sentiment, we have heard young skateboarders affirm that they "just want to get out there to skateboard and have fun." So be it for the sake of outdoors fun.

Figures 1.1 and 1.2 show TJ's photo in some of his fun skateboarding outings. The front cover of this book cogently demonstrates that a skateboarder and his skateboard are always the best of buddies.

Figure 1.1. TJ on a Skateboard Jump over concrete steps
(Courtesy TJ Photos)

Figure 1.2. TJ on a Skateboard Jump over a fire hydrant
(Courtesy TJ Photos)

Fellowship

Fellowship is the operative word among skateboarding enthusiasts. Unlike team sports, everybody at a skateboarding park is on the same team. The only opponents in skateboarding are physics and gravity, and everyone at the park wishes every other person success in triumphing over gravity. In fact, co-skaters often assist others in ensuring that success. Skateboarders even use nudging on and friendly dares to coax better performance out of fellow skaters. Figure 1.3 demonstrates the diversity of skateboarding fellowship, with each person doing his or her own thing under the watchful eyes of fellow skateboarders.

Figure 1.3. Skateboarding Fellowship of Independence at the park
© Can Stock Photo / nebojsa78

Following

The interest in skateboarding has growing steadily over the years. The incident of COVID-19 pandemic disrupted large gatherings in skateboarding parks all over the world, but the following is expected to rebound once the pandemic is eradicated through mass vaccination. The steady following of skateboarding has generated increased popularity across gender and age gaps. Enthusiasts openly or covertly pursue the fun and fellowship in shopping malls, parking lots, and side streets . . . regardless of whether or not "No Skateboarding" signs are posted. So widespread is the following of skateboarding that even man's best friend can join the fun of skateboarding. Figure 1.4 shows a happy dog skateboarding.

Skateboarding at the Olympics

Due to the worldwide growth of the following and acceptance of skateboarding, the sport has made it into the Olympics. It was slated to debut at the 2020 Olympics in Tokyo, Japan. Unfortunately, the COVID-19 pandemic upended the inaugural plans. It is, however, expected to be included in the postponed convenance of the Olympics in 2021.

Figure 1.4. Man's best friend, Happy Dog, skateboarding
(© CanStock Photo Madrabothair)

Educational Utility of Skateboarding

It has been reported that skateboarding has been declining over the past several years. This is probably because skateboarding is inherently a sport for youths, with more malleable, adaptive, and repairable born structures. As more and more skateboarders age out of the sport, the following is in danger of declining. Skateboard parks are less and less crowded. The COVID-19 pandemic and the ensuing lockdowns, reduction of large gatherings, and social distancing requirements did not help the case of skateboarding. For this reason, it is of interest to extend the attention of skateboarding from being just a sports pursuit to being an educational pursuit also. Hence, the focus of this book on the physics of skateboarding. If nothing else, readers can learn and enjoy the technical aspects of skateboarding.

Chapter 1 Bibliography for Further Reading

As motivational indication of the pervasiveness of studying the applications of science, technology, engineering, and technology (STEM) to sports, we present the selected bibliography below for the purpose of further exploration by readers.

1. Armenti, Angelo, Jr., editor (1992), **The Physics of Sports**, Springer-Verlag, New York, NY.
2. Badiru, Deji (2010), *The Physics of Soccer: Using Math and Science to Improve Your Game*, iUniverse, Bloomington, Indiana, USA.
3. Badiru, Deji (2014), *Youth Soccer Training Slides: A Math and Science Approach*, iUniverse, Bloomington, Indiana, USA.
4. Badiru, Deji (2018), *Physics of Soccer II: Science and Strategies for a Better Game*, iUniverse, Bloomington, Indiana, USA.
5. Badiru, Deji (2021), **Physics of Skateboarding: Fun, Fellowship, and Following**, iUniverse, Bloomington, Indiana, USA.
6. Barr, George (1990), **Sports Science for Young People**, Dover Publications, New York, NY.

7. Brody, Howard, Rod Cross, and Crawford Lindsey (2002), **The Physics and Technology of Tennis**, Racquet Tech Publishing, Solana Beach, CA.

8. Gallian, Joseph A., editor (2010), **Mathematics and Sports**, Mathematical Association of America, Washington, DC.

9. Gay, Timothy (2005), **The Physics of Football**, Harper Collins, New York, NY.

10. Goodstein, Madeline (2010), **GOAL! Science Projects with Soccer**, Enslow Publishers, Inc., Berkeley Heights, NJ.

11. Hache, Alain (2002), **The Physics of Hockey**, The John Hopkins University Press, Baltimore, MD.

12. Reilly, Thomas (2007), **The Science of Training – Soccer: A Scientific Approach to Developing Strength, Speed, and Endurance**, Routledge, New York, NY.

13. Sadovskii, L. E. and A. L. Sadovskii (1993), **Mathematics and Sports**, American Mathematical Society, Providence, RI.

14. Taylor, John (2014), **The Science of Soccer: A Bouncing Ball and a Banana Kick**, University of New Mexico Press, Albuquerque, NM.

15. Vizard, Frank (2008), **Why a Curveballs Curves: The incredible science of sports**, Hearst Books, New York, NY.

CHAPTER 2

WHEELS OF FUN

We should learn while having fun and have fun while learning. Everything we do is predicated on motion in one form or another. It's through physics that we reach out into space. Albert Einstein, the intellectual responsible for the most famous physics equation in history, said "Intellectual growth should commence at birth and cease only at death." This quote encourages continual learning about the world around us. Curiosity does not kill the cat; it makes the cat wiser. A better understanding of the applications of physics in our everyday lives provides an avenue for the intellectual growth that the quote urges us to embrace.

Physics, derived from the Greek word, physis (meaning "nature") is the natural science which explains fundamental concepts of mass, charge, matter, and its motion; as well as and all properties that arise from the concepts, such as energy, force, space, and time. Physics is the general analysis of nature, conducted in order to understand how the physical world behaves. Physics is a major player (pun intended) in STEM (Science, Technology, Engineering, and Mathematics) and it deserves a special treatment and understanding.

Principles of physics are embedded in or complemented by several other scientific bodies of knowledge such as astronomy, chemistry, mathematics, and biology. Because of this symbiotic relationship, the boundaries of physics remain difficult to distinguish. Physics is significant and influential because it provides an understanding of things that we see, observe, and use every day such as television, computers, cars, household appliances, and sports. The sports of skateboarding, in particular, is subject to many of the principles of physics.

Physics covers a wide range of phenomena of nature, from the smallest (e.g., sub-atomic particles) to the largest (e.g., galaxies). Included in this phenomena are the very basic objects from which all other things develop. It is because of this that physics is sometimes said to be the "fundamental science." Physics helps to describe the various phenomena that occur in nature in terms of easier-to-understand phenomena. Thus, physics aims to link the things we see around us to their origins or root causes. It then tries to link the root causes together in an attempt to find an ultimate reason for why nature is the way it is.

As examples, the ancient Chinese observed that certain rocks (i.e., lodestone) were attracted to one another by some invisible force. This effect was later called magnetism, and was first rigorously studied in the 17th century. A little earlier than the Chinese, the ancient Greeks knew of other objects such as amber, that when rubbed with fur, would cause a similar invisible attraction between the two. This was also first studied rigorously in the 17th century, and came to be called electricity. Thus, physics had come to understand two observations of nature in terms of some root cause (electricity and magnetism). However, further work in the 19th century revealed that these two forces were just two different aspects of one force – electromagnetism. This process of unifying or linking forces of nature continues today in contemporary studies of physics.

The major branches of physics related to different size-speed combinations of matter as summarized below:

Smaller size and lower speed: Quantum Mechanics
Larger size and lower speed: Classical Mechanics
Smaller size and higher speed: Quantum Field Theory
Larger size and higher speed: Relativistic Mechanics

Branch A: Classical mechanics. This deals with matter of large size and slow speed. Size is of the order far larger than 10-9 meters (e.g., ranging up to planetary sizes) while speed is of the order far less than 3x108 meters/second (e.g., speed of race bike).

Branch B: Quantum mechanics. This deals with matter of small size and small size. Size is of the order near or less than 10-9 meters (e.g., around sub-atomic level) while speed is of the order far less than 3x108 meters/second (e.g., speed of race bike).

Branch C: Quantum field theory. This branch deals with matter of small size and large speed. Size is of the order near or less than 10-9 meters (e.g., around sub-atomic level) while speed is of the order comparable to 3x108 meters/second (e.g., speed of light).

Branch D: Relativistic mechanics. This deals with matter of large size and large speed. Size is of the order far larger than 10-9 meters (e.g., ranging up to planetary sizes) while speed is of the order comparable to 3x108 meters/second (e.g., speed of light).

Scientific notation and conversion factors are important for the application of STEM to our day-to-day activities, including sports, such as skateboarding. It is essential that methods of evaluating measured data be understood so that quantities can be assessed and appreciated properly. As a good example, a news account in late September 1999 reported how the National Aeronautics and Space Administration (NASA) lost a $125 million Mars orbiter in a crash onto the surface of Mars because a Lockheed Martin engineering team used English units of measurement while the agency's team used the more conventional metric system for a key operation of the spacecraft. The unit's mismatch prevented navigation information from transferring between the Mars Climate Orbiter spacecraft team at Lockheed Martin in Denver and the flight team at NASA's Jet Propulsion Laboratory in Pasadena, California. A summary of metric conversion factors is presented in the appendix. Judging the distance, in whatever unit of measurement, from one point to the other on a skateboard routine is essential for making a safe landing. Figure 2.1 shows TJ in one of his gravity-defying leaps on a skateboard. In skateboarding, gravity can either aid or impede intended jump tricks. Mastering gravity is both an art and a science, arrived at through lengthy and dedicated practice.

Figure 2.1. TJ's Skateboard leap over a railing
(Courtesy TJ Photos)

CHAPTER 3

WORK AND ENERGY

This chapter presents some fundamentals of motion and energy that should be of interest to skateboarding followers. Energy is, indeed, a fascinating topic both from intellectual and usage standpoints. Even if, as engineers, we are already versed in the science of energy, new reinforcement in the social context of present energy crises will be informative. We must understand the inherent scientific characteristics of energy in order to fully appreciate the perilous future that we face if we don't act now. There are two basic forms of energy:

- Kinetic energy (due to motion)
- Potential energy (due to height off the ground)

Fancy skateboarding demonstrates mastery of how to leverage both kinetic and potential energies. All other forms of energy are derived from the kinetic and potential forms of energy. Energy that is stored (i.e., not being used) is potential energy. Energy transfer research enables us to understand how energy goes from one form to another.

Kinetic energy is found in anything that is in motion (e.g., waves, electrons, atoms, molecules, and physical objects).

Anything that moves produces kinetic energy, but what prompts it to move requires its own source of energy. Electrical energy is the movement of electrical charges. Radiant energy is electromagnetic energy traveling in waves. Radiant energy includes light, X-rays, gamma rays, and radio waves. Solar energy is an example of radiant energy. Motion energy is the movement of objects and substances from one place to another. Wind is an example of motion energy. Thermal or heat energy is the vibration and movement of matter (atoms and molecules inside a substance). Sound is a form of energy that moves in waves through a material. Sound is produced when a force causes an object to vibrate. The perception of sound is the sensing (picking up) of the vibration of an object.

Potential energy represents energy content by virtue of gravitational position as well as stored energy. For example, energy due to fuel, food, and elevation (gravity) represents potential energy. Chemical energy is energy derived from atoms and molecules contained in materials. Petroleum and natural gas are examples of chemical energy. Mechanical energy is the energy stored in a material by the application of force. Compressed springs and stretched rubber bands are examples of stored mechanical energy. Nuclear energy is stored in the nucleus of an atom. Gravitational energy is the energy of position and place. Water retained behind the wall of a dam is a demonstration of gravitational potential energy. Light is a form of energy that travels in waves. The light we see is referred to as visible light. However, there is also an invisible spectrum. Infrared or ultraviolet rays cannot be seen, but can be felt as heat. Sunburn is an example of the effect of infrared energy on the skin. The difference between visible and invisible light is the length of the radiation wave known as wavelengths. Radio waves have the longest rays while gamma rays have the shortest rays.

In summary, kinetic energy is the energy of moving objects. It depends on an object's mass and velocity.

$$KE = \frac{1}{2}mv^2$$

Where:
m = mass
v = velocity

Potential energy is the energy stored in an object located at a height above the Earth's surface. It depends on how high above the ground the object is positioned.

$$PE = mgh$$

Where:
m = mass
g = gravity
h = height above the ground

For trajectory motion, the potential energy at the top of the trajectory is equal to the kinetic energy at the bottom of the trajectory. The total energy of the trajectory system is kinetic energy plus potential energy. Work is the transfer of energy through mechanical means. It is the term used to describe how energy changes kinetic energy to potential energy. Work accomplished is equivalent to kinetic energy. It is important to note the following:

- When work is negative, kinetic energy decreases. For example, an upward movement of a skateboard implies a decrease in KE.

- When work is positive, kinetic energy increases. For example, a downward movement of a skateboard implies an increase in KE.

When we ordinarily talk about conserving energy, we often refer to reducing our consumption in order to save energy. Recalling Newton's law, energy cannot be created or destroyed. When energy is consumed, it does not disappear; it simply goes from one form to another. For example, solar energy cells change radiant energy into electrical energy. As an automobile engine burns gasoline (a form of chemical energy), it is transformed from the chemical form to a mechanical form. When energy is converted from one form to another, a useful portion of it is always lost because no conversion process is perfectly efficient. It is the objective of energy engineers to minimize that loss by putting the loss into another useful form. Therein lies the need to use science and engineering techniques to model the interaction of variables in an energy system mathematically in order to achieve optimized combination of energy resources for energy requirement of products, particularly new products.

One interesting energy theory is the conversion of kinetic energy to thermal energy (i.e., heat energy). This is comically presented in the "chicken-slapping cooking" theory of physics, in which a frozen chicken could, theoretically, be slapped hard for 100,000 thousand times to generate enough heat to cook the chicken. Interested readers can find multiple descriptions and examples in many Youtube postings online about this. There is even a mechanical contraption called "chicken slapper." The point is that energy can be converted from one form to another for useful purposes. Another common example is the generation of enough heat to start a fire by rubbing a rigid stick against a hard stone. In the same vein, a hard frictional force on a skateboard wheel could generate a damaging heat on the wheel.

In numeric terms, the kinetic energy of a body moving at velocity v meters/sec and with mass m kilogram is calculated as $1/2mv^2$ in Joules of energy. Readers should see the Appendix for the conversion factors between Joules and Watts of energy. It is not our purpose or expertise to teach physics in this book, but to provide enough motivational interest for readers to seek a deeper knowledge (elsewhere) for the specific topics of interest to them.

Energy in the Universe

It is a physical fact that there is abundant energy in the world. Use of the resource is just a matter of meeting technical requirements to convert it into useful and manageable forms from one source to another. For example, every second, the sun converts 600 million tons of hydrogen into 596 million tons of helium through nuclear fusion. The remaining 4 million tons of hydrogen is converted into energy in accordance with Einstein's theory of relativity, which famously states that:

$$E = mc^2,$$

where E represents energy, m represents mass of matter, and c represents speed of light. This equation says that energy and mass are equivalent and transmutable. That is, they are fundamentally the same thing. The equation confirms that a very large amount of energy can be released quickly from an extremely small amount of matter; the right matter for that matter. This is why atomic weapons are so powerful and effective. The theory of relativity is also the basic principle behind the way the sun gives off energy, by converting matter into energy. What the sun produces is a lot of energy that equates to 40,000 watts per square inch on the visible surface of the sun. This can be effectively harnessed for use on Earth; and it accounts for the ongoing push to install more solar systems to meet our energy needs.

Although the Earth receives only one-half of a billionth of the sun's energy, this still offers sufficient potential for harnessing. Comprehensive technical, quantitative, and qualitative analysis will be required to achieve widespread harnessing around the world. Industrial engineering and operations research can play an important role in that energy pursuit. The future of energy will involve several decisions involving technical and managerial issues such as the following:

- Point-of-use generation
- Co-generation systems
- Micro-power generation systems
- Energy supply transitions
- Coordination of energy alternatives
- Global energy competition
- Green-power generation systems
- Integrative harnessing of sun, wind, and water energy sources
- Energy generation, transformation, transmission, distribution, storage, and consumption across global boundaries
- Socially-responsible negawatt systems (i.e., to invest in reducing electricity demand instead of investing to increase electricity generation capacity).

All of the above details about energy are important for sports just as they are for all other human pursuits. The more skateboarders appreciate these details, the more they would be ready to be more socially responsible users of energy. Even the minuscule issue of conserving energy while playing does have long-term implications in the overall scheme of our existence.

The universe offers tremendous amounts of natural energy, albeit over vast distances. Light, in its various spectra, form the basis for a lot of the energy in the universe. Light travels fast and vast to bring us live-supporting energy on Earth.

Speed of light $\approx$ 299,792,458 meters per second
$\approx$ 186,000 miles per second
$\approx$ 669,600,000 miles per hour

Speed of sound $\approx$ 340.29 meters per second
$\approx$ 0.211446403 miles per second
$\approx$ 761.207051 miles per hour

Conversion factors are presented in the Appendix. Online reference materials and other published sources provide extensive information about the speed of light. The term *speed of light* refers to the speed of light in a vacuum (i.e., free space). This is a fundamental physical constant usually denoted by the symbol c. It is the speed of all electromagnetic radiation, including visible light. The speed of light in a vacuum is *exactly* 299,792,458 m/s.

A light-year is the distance light travels in one year. Thus, at the speed noted above, one light-year translates to 5,878,499,810,000 miles traveled by light in one year. That is,

$$1 \text{ light-year} = 5.87849981 \times 10^{12} \text{ miles}$$
$$1 \text{ light-year} = 9.4605284 \times 10^{12} \text{ kilometers}$$

Celestial objects that are rated as being so many light-years away represent vast distances travelled by light before we can observe those objects on Earth. In specific cases, celestial lights that we observe on Earth at this point in time actually started traveling from the emitting objects millions of years ago, before reaching us now for present-day observation. Imagine an object in a galaxy that is 50 million light-years away. What we see now occurred 50 million years ago in that galaxy. To put things in perspective, what is happening on a distant star right now won't be observed on Earth for millions of years into the future. The speed of light is a fundamental constant of space and time. No matter or information can travel faster than the speed of light.

For many practical purposes, the speed of light is so great that it can be regarded as instantaneous travel. An exception is where long distances or precise time measurements are involved. For example, in the global positioning system (GPS), a GPS receiver measures its distance to satellites based on how long it takes for a radio signal to arrive from the satellite. In astronomy, distances are often measured in light-years, which is explained above.

It should be noted that the speed of light when it passes through a transparent or translucent material medium, like glass or air, is less than its speed in a vacuum. The speed is inversely proportional to the refractive index of the medium. In specially prepared media, the speed can be very small or even zero. If a projectile or spacecraft is sent upward with an initial speed of 11.2 km/s (25,200 MPH or 7 miles per second), it would leave the Earth. This is called the "escape velocity" from Earth's surface.

To put relative speeds into perspective, consider the speed of the blink of an eye. We often hear of comparisons to what happens "in the blink of an eye." For example, cars on a highway race past a mile marker in the blink of an eye, or a fast player zooms by an opponent in the blink of an eye. Well, the average blink generally lasts between 300 and 400 milliseconds. That is, three tenths to four tenths of a second. How fast is this on a miles-per-hour scale? This is an interesting exercise left to the calculation and imagination skills of readers. In solving this riddle, consider the distance covered by a blink within its four-tenths-of-a-second speed rating. What about the speed of a wink? After all, a wink could be a form of covert communication among fellow skateboarders during a skateboard rally.

Principles of Simple Machines

Mechanically, simple machines are used for accomplishing work. In skateboarding, the skateboard and ramps work in cohesion to do the desired work of moves and jumps. With physics, there are ways of making work easier. The most common tools for accomplishing work fall in the category of six simple machines that are listed below and shown in Figure 3.1:

1. The Lever
2. The Wheel and Axle
3. The Pulley
4. The Inclined Plane
5. The Wedge
6. The Screw

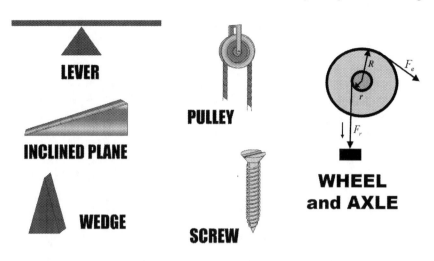

Figure 3.1: Simple Machines

For skateboarding purposes, the lever and the inclined plane (ramp) are the most commonly used. All machines, no matter how large or complex, are made up of combinations of the six simple machines. Although they all may not be directly applicable to skateboarding, the six simple machines help to emphasize the importance of physics in our everyday activities.

A machine is a tool that enables a force to be applied at a certain point by the application of another force at a different point. Machines are usually designed so that a small effort may overcome a large load. For example, a ball juggler may be able to juggle a ball effortlessly, controlling the ball in impossible ways through the application of the principles of simple machines. Won't it be a thing of beauty to have skateboarder juggle a ball while skateboarding? It sounds impossible, but we have seen determined people do seemingly impossible things in sports.

The ratio of load to effort is called mechanical advantage (MA). That is, the mechanical advantage is the ratio of the force of resistance to the force of effort. This is represented by the equation below, which is available from various published physics books.

$$MA = \frac{F_R}{F_E}$$

Where:

MA = mechanical advantage

F_R = force of resistance (N)

F_R = force of effort (N)

The mechanical advantage is the factor by which a machine multiplies the force put into it. The efficiency of a machine is given by the ratio of "useful work done by the machine" to the "work done on the machine." That is, efficiency (*e*) is defined as:

$$e = \frac{\text{work output of a machine}}{\text{work input to the machine}}.$$

A perfect machine has an efficiency of 1. Actual machines have efficiencies much less than 1. Velocity ratio of a machine is the ratio defined as:

$$vr = \frac{\text{distance that the effort moves}}{\text{distance that the load moves}}$$

where "distance that the effort moves" represents the amount of effort applied in a particular direction and "distance that the load moves" represents how far the subject of the effort moves in a particular direction.

The Lever

A lever consists of a rigid bar that is free to turn on a pivot, which is called a fulcrum. The lever is a bar supported at a single point, the fulcrum. The positioning of the fulcrum changes the mechanical advantage of the lever. For example, by placing the fulcrum at a certain point, we may be able to lift a 200-pound weight with the application of a force of only 100 pounds. In ancient Egypt, builders used the principle of levers to move and position stone pillars weighing more than 100 tons. Greek mathematician Archimedes (*c.* 287 BC to *c.* 212 BC) is reported to have said, "Give me the place to stand, and I shall move the earth." The respective distances and forces are represented as D1, D2, F1, and F2, respectively.

When a lever is in static equilibrium (i.e., balanced), the following mathematical relationship holds:

$$\mathbf{F_1 D_1 = F_2 D_2}$$

The effort arm represents where force is input. The effort arm is always larger than the resistance arm. The force applied at end points of the lever is proportional to the ratio of the length of the lever arm measured between the fulcrum and application point of the force applied at each end of the lever. Mathematically, this is expressed by M = Fd. There are three classes of levers representing variations in the location of the fulcrum and the input and output forces. The mechanical advantage is also calculated as shown previously.

Examples of first-class levers:

1. Seesaw (also known as a teeter-totter)
2. Crowbar
3. Pliers (double lever)
4. Scissors (double lever)
5. Flip (e.g., flipping a skateboard using a rigid bar)

Examples of second-class levers:

1. Wheelbarrow
2. Nutcracker (double lever)
3. The handle of a pair of nail clippers
4. An oar
5. Lift (e.g., balancing a skateboard on the instep and raising it by tilting the foot using the heel as the fulcrum, before jumping on the skateboard)

Examples of third-class levers:

1. Human arm
2. Tongs (double lever) (where hinged at one end, the style with a central pivot is first-class)
3. Catapult
4. Any number of tools, such as a hoe or scythe
5. The main body of a pair of nail clippers in which the handle exerts the incoming force

The Wheel and Axle

A "wheel and axle" consists of a large wheel attached to an axle so that both turn together. Any large disk (the wheel) attached to a small-diameter shaft or rod (the axle) can provide mechanical advantage for performing work. Turning a screw with a screwdriver is a simple example of a wheel and axle. The fundamental equation of wheel and axle is shown below:

$$F_R \cdot r_R \cdot = F_E \cdot r_E,$$

where

F_R = force of resistance (N)

F_E = force of effort (N)

r_R = radius of resistance wheel (m)

r_E = radius of effort wheel (m)

The mechanical advantage for a wheel and axle is represented as shown below:

$$MA_{\text{wheel and axle}} = \frac{r_E}{r_R}$$

This is the ratio of the radius of the wheel to the radius of the axle. If the radius of the wheel is four times greater than the radius of the axle, every time we turn the wheel once, the force applied will be multiplied four times. Examples of wheel and axles include bicycles, Ferris wheels, gears, wrenches, doorknobs, and steering wheels.

The Pulley

A pulley is any rope or cable looped around a support. A very simple pulley system would be a rope thrown over a branch to hoist something into the air. Often, pulleys incorporate a wheel and axle system to reduce the friction on the rope and the support.

If a pulley is fastened to a fixed object, it is called a "fixed pulley." If the pulley is fastened to the resistance to be moved, it is called a "moveable pulley." When one continuous cord is used, the ratio reduces according to the number of strands holding the resistance in the pulley system. The effort force equals the tension in each supporting stand. The mechanical advantage of the pulley is given by the following formula:

$$MA_{pulley} = \frac{F_R}{F_E} = \frac{nT}{T} = n$$

where
T = tension in each supporting strand
n = number of strands holding the resistance
F_R = force of resistance
F_E = force of effort

The Inclined Plane

An inclined plane is a surface set at an angle from the horizontal and used to raise objects that are too heavy to lift vertically. Often referred to as a *ramp*, the inclined plane allows us to multiply the applied force over a longer distance. In other words, we exert less force but for a longer distance. The same amount of work is done, but it just seems easier because it is spread over time.

If an object is put on an inclined plane, it will move if the force of friction is smaller than the combined force of gravity and normal force. If the angle of the inclined plane is 90 degrees (rectangle), the object will free fall. A ramp is an example of an inclined plane for skateboarding purposes. In ball juggling routine, for example, a skillful skateboarder, standing on a skateboard, can use his or her outstretched leg and thigh as a ramp to roll the ball down onto his foot before flipping the ball into a juggling routine, while rolling downhill on a skateboard. Figure 3.2 shows a caricature of a skateboarder on an inclined plane (a ramp). The mechanical advantage of an inclined plane is:

$$MA_{\text{inclined plane}} = \frac{F_R}{F_E} = \frac{1}{h},$$

where
F_R = force of resistance (N)
R_E = force of effort (N)
l = length of plane (m)
h = height of plane (m)

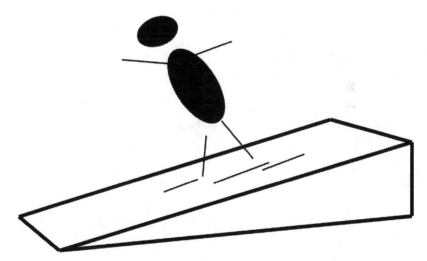

Figure 3.2. Caricature of a skateboarder on an inclined plane

The Wedge

A wedge works in a similar way to the inclined plane, only it is forced into an object to prevent it from moving or to split it into pieces. A knife is a common use of the wedge. Other examples are axes, forks, nails, and door wedges. The wedge is a modification of the inclined plane. The mechanical advantage of a wedge can be found by dividing the length of either slope by the thickness of the longer end.

As with the inclined plane, the mechanical advantage gained by using a wedge requires a corresponding increase in distance. The mechanical advantage is calculated by the expression below:

$$MA = \frac{s}{T},$$

where
MA = mechanical advantage
s = length of either slope (m)
T = thickness of the longer end (m)

Wedges are used as either separating or holding devices. A wedge can be composed of either one or two inclined planes. A double wedge can be thought of as two inclined planes joined together with their surfaces sloping outward.

The Screw

A screw is an inclined plane wrapped around a circle or rod. A screw can be used to move a load (like a corkscrew) or to split and separate an object (like a carpenter's screw). From the law of machines, we have the following equation:

$$F_R \cdot h = F_E \cdot U_E$$

For advancing a screw with a screwdriver, the mechanical advantage is given by the equation below:

$$MA_{\text{screw}} = \frac{F_R}{F_E} = \frac{U_E}{h},$$

where
F_R = force of resistance (N)
F_E = effort force (N)
h = pitch of screw
U_E = circumference of the handle of the screw

A comprehensive pursuit of the fun, fellowship, and following of skateboarding will make use of the six simple machines in one form or another.

CHAPTER 4

NEWTON'S LAWS OF MOTION

No technical discussion of sports will be complete without a mention or basic understanding of Newton's Laws of Motion. Motion is the basis of executing skateboarding routines. Skateboarding is a sport of constant motion. Even when motion is temporarily suspended at a stationary point in an aerial routine, the instantaneous equal and opposite forces still come into play. The principles of physics are crucial in understanding the characteristics of a body in motion, be it the skateboard or a skateboarder's body mass. The movements of a ball and a player are analogous to the movements of a skateboarder and his or her skateboard.

Recalling the adage of "a fool and his goal are soon parted," we can consider a lack of understanding of the laws of motion as being responsible for the parting of the skateboarder and his skateboard. If motion analysis is well understood, either through practice or study, the skateboard could be kept within the reach of the human counterpart (i.e., skateboarder) at all times.

Mechanics deals with the relations of force, matter, and motion. This chapter deals with the mathematical methods of describing motion. This computational branch of mechanics is called kinematics. *Motion* is defined as a continuous change of position. In most actual motions, different points in a body move along different paths. The complete motion can be understood if we know how each point in the body moves. We can consider only a moving point in a body or a very small body called a particle. The position of a particle is specified by its projections onto the three axes of a rectangular coordinate system. As the particle moves along any path in space, its projections move in straight lines along the three axes. The actual motion can be reconstructed from the motions of these three projections.

Biomechanics is the application of mechanical principles to living organisms. This is particularly important for the practice of sports medicine, where issues of concern include joint instability, design of sports-assistive devices, lower extremity functions, and gait and posture analysis. In effect, biomechanics is a field that combines the disciplines of biology and engineering mechanics and utilizes the tools of physics, mathematics, and engineering to quantitatively describe the properties of biological constituents of living organisms. For example, biomechanics analyzes the internal and external forces acting on the human body (e.g., a skateboarder) and the effects produced by the forces.

If we consider a particle moving along the x-axis, we can plot its x coordinate as a function of time, t. The displacement of a particle as it moves from one point of its path to another is defined as the vector Δx drawn from the first point to the second point. Thus, the vector from P to Q, of magnitude $x_2 - x_1 = \Delta x$, is the displacement. The *average velocity* of the particle is then defined as the ratio of the displacement to the time interval $t_2 - t_1 = \Delta t$. We can represent average velocity by the equation below:

$$\bar{v} = \frac{\Delta x}{\Delta t}.$$

The purpose here is not to overwhelm the reader with intricate details of kinematics; but rather to pique the interest of young readers in understanding that there is some scientific principle behind what happens in movements on the skateboard. More advanced readers can consult regular physics textbooks to get the computational details at whatever level they desire.

Newton's First Law of Motion

Sir Isaac Newton, a seventeenth-century scientist, developed laws to explain why objects move or don't move. These are known as Newton's laws of motion. Newton's first law of motion, also known as the law of inertia, says the following:

An object at rest tends to stay at rest and an object in motion tends to stay in motion with the same speed and in the same direction unless acted upon by an unbalanced force. Figure 4.1 shows a balancing of a skateboard on a beam.

Figure 4.1. TJ's Skateboard Balancing on a beam (an object at rest)
(Courtesy TJ Photos)

What is a force? A force is a directional push or pull upon an object resulting from the object's interaction with another object. Force is that which changes or tends to change the state of rest or uniform motion of an object. Whenever there is an interaction between two objects, there is a force upon each of them. When the interaction ceases, the two objects no longer experience the force. Forces exist as a result of an interaction between objects. There are two broad categories of force:

1.   Contact force
2.   Action-at-a-distance force

Contact forces result from physical contact (interaction) between two objects. Examples include the following:

- Frictional force
- Tensional force
- Normal force
- Air resistance force
- Spring force
- Applied force

Action-at-a-distance forces result even when two interacting objects are not in physical contact with each other, but are still able to exert a push or pull on each other. Examples include the following:

- Gravitational force
- Electrical force
- Magnetic force

Force is a quantity that is measured using the standard metric unit known as the *newton* (N). One newton is the amount of force required to give a 1-kilogram mass an acceleration of 1 m/s/s. Thus, the following unit equivalency can be stated:

$$1 \text{ Newton} = 1 \text{kg} \frac{m}{s^2}$$

A force is a vector quantity. A vector is a quantity that has both magnitude and direction. To fully describe the force acting upon an object, we must describe both the magnitude (size or numerical value) and the direction.

Newton's Second Law of Motion

Newton's second law of motion states that the acceleration of an object as produced by a net force is directly proportional to the magnitude of the net force, in the same direction as the net force, and inversely proportional to the mass of the object. This law is expressed by the following equation:

$$F = ma,$$

where F is the net force acting on the object. This equation sets the net force equal to the product of the mass times the acceleration. Acceleration (a) is the rate of change of velocity (v), and velocity is the rate of change of distance. Figure 4.2 demonstrates how force, mass, and acceleration could be used to an advantage for skateboarding.

Figure 4.2. Force, mass, and acceleration in a skateboard drum jump
(Courtesy TJ Photos)

Newton's first law of motion predicts the behavior of objects for which all existing forces are balanced. The first law states that if the forces acting upon an object are balanced, then the acceleration of that object will be 0 m/s/s. Objects at equilibrium (i.e., forces are balanced) will not accelerate. An object is said to be in equilibrium when the resultant force acting on it is 0. For three forces to be in equilibrium, the resultant of any two of the forces must be equal and opposite to the third force. According to Newton, an object will accelerate only if there is a net or unbalanced force acting upon it. The presence of an unbalanced force on an object will accelerate it, thus changing its speed, its direction, or both.

By comparison, Newton's second law of motion pertains to the behavior of objects for which all existing forces are *not* balanced. The second law states that the acceleration of an object is dependent upon two variables: the net force acting upon the object and the mass of the object. The acceleration of an object depends directly upon the net force acting upon the object, and inversely upon the mass of the object. As the force acting upon an object is increased, the acceleration of the object is increased. As the mass of an object is increased, the acceleration of the object is decreased.

Newton's Third Law of Motion

Newton's third law of motion states that for every action, there is an equal and opposite reaction. A force is a push or a pull upon an object that results from its interaction with another object. Forces result from interactions between objects. According to Newton, whenever objects A and B interact with each other, they exert forces upon each other. When a skateboarder sits

40

in a chair, his body exerts a downward force on the chair, and the chair exerts an upward force on his body. There are two forces resulting from this interaction: a force on the chair and a force on the body. These two forces are called *action* and *reaction* forces in Newton's third law of motion. One key thing to remember is that inanimate objects, such as walls, can push and pull back on an object, such as a skateboarding beam (see Figure 4.3).

Figure 4.3. Action and Reaction skateboard photo
(Courtesy TJ Photos)

The longer a force acts on an object, the faster the object will move. When kicking a ball, the longer the foot stays in contact with the ball, the faster the ball will move. This is called "follow-through." It makes the force act longer on the ball to make it go faster. It is common to see good players in golf and tennis continue their swings as long as possible. Similarly, good baseball batters take long swings. Other examples include hammer throwers in track, who swing around several times before letting go, and javelin throwers, who hold on as long as possible by making a complete about-face before releasing the javelin.

The principle of *force duration* is applied in reverse when a force slows down an object. The longer a force acts on an object to slow it down, the more effective and smoother the stopping effect. Thus, when a good ball player receives a fast pass, the ball is brought under control more effectively by elongating the duration of the stopping force. This is accomplished by drawing the foot back as the ball makes contact with the foot. This technique increases the time that the slowing-down force acts on the ball. This way, the ball does not strike the foot with too much sudden impact. This approach lessens the possibility of the ball ricocheting off uncontrollably. When this is executed very well, the ball control is a thing of beauty to watch.

The best display of reverse force-duration skill witnessed by the first author was by a high school player at Saint Finbarr's College in Nigeria in 1972. A high ball was descending on the field of play. The player jumped up vertically and connected with the ball about six feet above the ground. As gravity pulled the player back toward the ground, he and the ball came down at the same speed, with the ball resting still on top of his foot. They both reached the ground together, whence he smoothly put the ball back into play on the ground. Similar demonstrations are often displayed by skateboarders during skateboard jumps.

Shoulder-to-shoulder outmuscling an opponent is allowed in some sports. To accomplish this, a player must build strength to apply a force in accordance with Newton's laws of motion. What happens in this case is force application (action) in one direction that is countered by a reaction (push back) in the other direction. If one force exceeds the other, both bodies move in the direction of the higher force.

Centripetal and Centrifugal Forces

Two types of forces that are of interest are centripetal and centrifugal forces. Centripetal force is in effect when an object is in circular motion. Any motion in a curved path involves a force that tends to pull the object toward the center of curvature of the path. *Centripetal* force means "center-seeking" force. The force has the magnitude expressed as shown below:

$$\mathbf{F}_{CP} = m\frac{v^2}{r}$$

Where:
m = mass of the object
v = velocity of the object
r = radius of the circle making up the curved path
v^2/r represents the centripetal acceleration

From the above equation, the centripetal force is proportional to the square of the velocity. This means that a doubling of speed will require four times the centripetal force to keep the object moving on a circular path. If the centripetal force must be provided by friction alone on a curve, an increase in speed could lead to an unexpected skid if friction is insufficient. This explains why a car can skid tangentially off the road when speeding through a curve. Similarly, a mass swinging circularly on a string requires tension in the string. The mass will travel off in a tangential straight line if the string breaks.

Centrifugal force is the converse of centripetal force, as it represents a force that tends to move an object away from the center of its circular path. *Centrifugal* force is a "center-avoiding" force; it is derived from Latin *centrum* ("center") and *fugere* ("to flee"). Objects in a circular rotational frame appear to be under the influence of an outwardly radial force that is proportional to the distance from the axis of rotation and to the rate of rotation of the frame.

Centrifugal force supposedly arises due to the inherent property of mass (also known as inertia), but many physicists do not consider it as a real force. For the purpose of our skateboarding scientific reasoning here, we will accept it as an imaginary force. Inertia represents the reluctance of a body to change either its speed or direction. According to Newton's laws of motion, a body that is at rest will stay at rest until some force makes it move, and then it will continue to move at the same speed and in the same direction until some force makes it move differently. We may mistakenly think that centrifugal force is what makes an object on a turning car's dashboard slide in a direction opposite the curved path of the car. But the real reason the object slides on the car's dash is because it wants to remain in a straight line (Newton's first law) while the car is turning. This same reasoning is why a little kid may have fun on a school bus sliding on the seat, if there is no restraining seat belt, as the bus goes around sharp turns while the body wants to go in a straight path.

With respect to forces that act on a speeding object, the reader is given the following challenge assignment to be researched and discussed with family members, friends, or classmates: What makes a speeding car go airborne in an accident?

Mass and Weight

The mass of an object is an inherent property of the object that conveys the amount of matter contained in the object. Mass is a fundamental property that is hard to define in terms of something else. Any physical quantities can be defined in terms of mass, length, and time. Mass is normally considered to be an unchanging property of an object. The usual symbol for mass is m, and its SI unit is the kilogram. The weight (w) of an object is the force of gravity on the object and may be defined as the mass times the acceleration of gravity (g), as shown below:

$$w = mg$$

Since the weight is a force, its SI unit is the newton. Density is defined as:

$$\text{Density} = \frac{\text{Mass}}{\text{Volume}}$$

Curving an Object

Can a skateboarder execute a "banana jump?" This is an interesting proposition that is analogous to curving the ball in baseball or soccer. David Beckham is reputed to be able to bend (curve) the ball to throw off defenders and the goalie. The process of curving the ball, well known as the banana kick, uses many of the principles of physics. Execution of the kick is both an art and science. The science part of the execution involves wind speed and direction. The art of it is being able to accurately judge the prevailing environmental conditions and adapt the kick to take advantage of those conditions. While the science of wind shear can be taught, what is even more important are innate good judgment and dedicated practice sessions. That is why some players can execute this kick while others cannot. In order to achieve a banana kick, the ball is not kicked along the line of the center but rather across the ball with a twisting flick of the foot. The result is a spin on the ball that sends the ball on a trajectory often difficult for opponents to guess or defend. Maybe with this interesting proposition or challenge, skateboarders will start practicing and executing a new type of jump trick called a "banana jump."

Pressure and Spinning

Spinning is of great interest and importance in many sports. Complex physics occurs whenever an object spins. Even a skateboard is subject to spinning in a skateboard routine. Forces act on the object in all directions. When all forces are perfectly balanced, the object is stationary. Superiority of a force in one direction causes motion in that direction. The Magnus effect is normally used to explain the movements of spinning objects. There are three general forces that act on the flight of an object:

1. Gravity
2. Drag
3. Magnus force

The Magnus force can be described in terms of an imbalance in the drag forces on a ball. The force was known about for centuries, but it was formally described in 1852 by the German physicist, Heinrich Magnus. Earlier, in 1742, a British artillery engineer, Benjamin Robins, had explained deviations in the trajectories of musket balls in terms of this effect. The schematic below demonstrates the Magnus force acting on a spinning ball.

Spinning is dependent on pressure difference. The effect of pressure difference accounts for many phenomena that we observe or experience. For example, when you drink a liquid with a straw, you create a low pressure inside the straw by sucking air out of it toward the inside of your mouth. The lower pressure (vacuum) created inside the straw forces the liquid, which is under a higher ambient pressure, up the straw and into your mouth. If, when the liquid is halfway up the straw, you block the end of the straw with your tongue, the liquid stays up inside the straw. This is because blocking the straw creates a balance of pressure on either side of the liquid. This causes it to become stationary.

When a ball is spinning in the air, it creates a boundary layer around itself, and the boundary layer induces a more widespread circular motion of the air. If the body is moving through the air with a velocity V, the velocity of the air close to the ball is a little greater than V on one side, and a little less than V on the other. This is because the induced velocity due to the boundary layer surrounding the spinning ball is added to V on one side, and subtracted from V on the other. In accordance with Bernoulli's principle, the velocity is greater when the wind pressure is less; and where the velocity is less, the wind pressure is greater. This pressure gradient results in a net force on the ball and creates subsequent motion in a direction perpendicular to the relative velocity vector (i.e., the velocity of the ball relative to the air flow).

The mathematical theorem called the Kutta-Joukowski theorem relates the lift generated by a right cylinder to the speed of the cylinder through a fluid or air, the density of the fluid or air, and the circulation of the fluid or air. The equation below calculates the lift force generated by inducing physical rotation on an object.

$$F = \frac{1}{2} \rho wr VAl$$

Where:
F = lift force
ρ = density of the fluid
w = angular velocity
r = radius of the object (if round)
V = velocity of the object
A = cross-sectional area of the object (if round)
l = lift coefficient

The lift coefficient may be determined from plots of experimental data. The spin ratio of the object is defined by the equation below:

$$\text{Spin ratio} = \frac{(Angular\ velocity)(Diameter)}{2(Linear\ velocity)}$$

For a smooth ball with a spin ratio of 0.5 to 4.5, typical lift coefficients range from 0.2 to 0.6.

It is clear that the duration of a force affects motion. The longer a force acts on an object to speed it up, the faster the object will move. The skateboarder's weight, arm stretching, leg extending, couching, body bending, squatting, and so on all generate force components that contribute to the overall skateboarding moves and tricks. May the force be with the skateboarder!

CHAPTER 5

MOTION AND CALCULATIONS

Movement and control of the skateboard and skateboarder in unison requires a coordination of the fundamental principles of motion and geometrical calculations. For experienced skateboarders, this becomes second nature, through extensive practice, without explicit calculations. Nonetheless, novice skateboarders may find it interesting and motivational to see some of the underlying principles and calculations. That is the purpose of this chapter. Some of the computational examples are drawn from other sports other than skateboarding.

Just as it is with many land-space-based sports, a basic appreciation of geometrical patterns is very important for skateboarding. From the construction of the geometry of the skateboard ramp to the layout of skateboarding track routing, geometry plays a direct part in the path. Figure 5.1 illustrates an example of the geometrical impact of the surface of a skateboard ramp.

Figure 5.1. Geometry of Skateboard Ramp
(Courtesy TJ Photos)

Bisection of Angles

In the images in Figure 5.2, $x = 60$ and $y = 40$. If the dashed lines bisect the angles with measures of $x°$ and $y°$, what is the value of z?

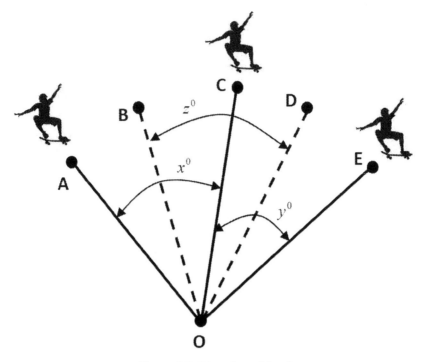

Figure 5.2. Bisection of Angles

A. 25
B. 35
C. 40
D. 45
E. 50

Answer: E
First, add the labeled points A, B, C, D, E, and O to the figure, as shown below. Then segment $\overline{OB}$ bisects $\angle AOC$, so $m\angle AOB$ = $m\angle BOC$, and $m\angle AOB + m\angle BOC = x° = 60°$. Thus, $m\angle AOB$ = $m\angle BOC = 30°$. Similarly, $m\angle COD = m\angle DOE = 20°$, because $\angle COD$ and $\angle DOE$ are of equal measure and the sum of their measures is $y° = 40°$. From the figure, it follows that $z° =$ $m\angle BOC + m\angle COD = 30° + 20° = 50°$. Therefore, $z = 50$.

Line Segment Comparison

Although a line segment is check-marked sequentially at points A, B, C, D, and E and we are given the following relationships: $AB < BC < CD < DE$, which of the following must be true based on the line segment relationships?

A. $AC < CD$
B. $AC < CE$
C. $AD < CE$
D. $AD < DE$
E. $BD < DE$

Answer: B

You can rewrite AC as $AB + BC$, AD as $AB + BC + CD$, CE as $CD + DE$, and BD as $BC + CD$, and then consider the five answers. The first choice is equivalent to $AB + BC$ is less than CD. You know that AB is less than CD and that BC is also less than CD, but the sum of AB and BC might not be less than CD. Since the question asks which statement *must* be true, the first choice is not the correct answer.

The second choice is equivalent to $AB + BC$ is less than $CD + DE$. This statement must be true, because AB is less than CD and BC is less than DE. Although there is no need to consider the other answers once you see that the second choice must be true, each of the remaining choices could be rewritten in the same way, and you could see that they need not be true.

Rectangle Length Comparison

The length of rectangle *S* is 20 percent longer than the length of rectangle *R*, and the width of rectangle *S* is 20 percent shorter than the width of rectangle *R*. Based on this information, the area of rectangle *S* can be inferred to be:

A. 20 percent greater than the area of rectangle *R*
B. 4 percent greater than the area of rectangle *R*
C. Equal to the area of rectangle *R*
D. 4 percent less than the area of rectangle *R*
E. 20 percent less than the area of rectangle *R*

Answer: D

Let's represent the length and width of rectangle *R* as *x* and *y*. Then the area of *R* is *xy*. The length of rectangle *S* is 20 percent longer than *x*, which is $x + 0.20x$, or $1.2x$. Similarly, the width of *S* is $y - 0.20y$, or $0.8y$. The area of *S* is $(1.2x)(0.8y)$, which simplifies to $0.96xy$. From this it follows that the area of rectangle *S* is 4 percent less than the area of rectangle *R*.

Rectangle within Practice Circle

In Figure 5.3, Point A marks the center of the practice circle from where skateboarding practice runs originate while Points B, C, D, and E mark the positional options for intermediate turns and spins. Point B is twelve feet from A and Points A, B, C, and D are located at the corners of a rectangle. Point E is eighteen feet from B. How long is line segment BD?

A: 18 feet
B: 20 feet
C: 30 feet
D: 12 feet
E: 42 feet

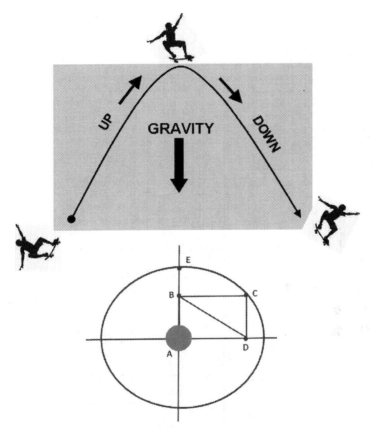

Figure 5.3. Rectangle within Practice Circle

Answer: C

Note that the shape ABCD forms a rectangle. Thus, BD and AC must be the same length, representing the diagonal of the rectangle. But AC also represents the radius of the practice circle. Thus, AE and BD are equal. Based on the given data that AB is twelve feet and BE is eighteen feet, the radius of the circle is twelve feet + eighteen feet = thirty feet. Consequently, BD = thirty feet.

Line Segments

A, B, C, and *D* are points on a line, with *D* the midpoint of segment BC. The lengths of segments AB, AC, and BC are 10, 2, and 12, respectively. What is the length of segment AD?

A. 2
B. 4
C. 6
D. 10
E. 12

Answer: B

Solution Steps

The key to this question lies in *not* jumping to incorrect conclusions. The question names the points on a line. It gives us a variety of information about the points. The one thing it *does not* do is tell us the order in which the points fall. Some may assume that the order of the points is *A*, then *B*, then *C*, then *D*. But as we will see, if we try to locate the points in this order, we will not be able to answer the question.

Points of Interest

The question asks for the length of line segment AD. In order to find this length, we have to establish the relative positions of the four points on the line.

Given Data

Drawing the figure would help as shown in Figure 5.4. We might be tempted to locate point *A* first. Unfortunately, we don't yet have enough information about *A* to place it correctly.

We can place *B, C,* and *D* because *D* is the midpoint in Figure 5.4 (a).

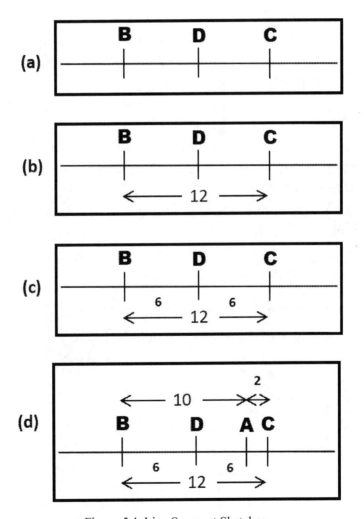

Figure 5.4. Line Segment Sketches

We know the lengths of three of the line segments:

AB = 10

AC = 2

BC = 12

Because we know where BC is located, we can label the length of BC (Figure 5.4 (b)).

Now, construct the figure by adding what we know and what we can figure out. Because *D* is the midpoint of BC, we know that BD and DC are each 6 units long (Figure 5.4(c)).

Where can we place point *A*? It has to be 2 units from *C*, because AC = 2. It also has to be 10 units from *B*, because AB = 10. So, the only location for *A* is between *B* and *C*, but closer to *C*. Place point *A* and mark the distances. We can now figure out the answer to the question. DC is 6 units. *A* is 2 units closer to *D* than *C*, so AD is 4 units (Figure 5.4 (d)).

Size of Line Segment

In triangle ABC, the length of side BC is 2 and the length of side AC is 12. Which of the following could be the length of side AB?

A. 6
B. 8
C. 10
D. 12
E. 14

Answer: D

By the triangle inequality, the sum of the lengths of any two sides of a triangle must be greater than the length of the remaining side. So, BC + AB > AC or 2 + AB > 12. Thus, AB > 10, which eliminates options (A), (B), and (C). Also, by the triangle inequality, BC + AC > AB, or 14 > AB, which eliminates option (E). Therefore, only option D, 12, could be the length of a side.

Triangle Overlap with Circle

The circle shown in Figure 5.5 has center O and a radius of length 5. If the area of the shaded region is 20, what is the value of x?

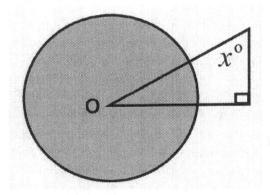

Figure 5.5: Triangle overlap with circle

A. 18
B. 36
C. 45
D. 54
E. 72

Answer: A

Solution

In order to find the value of *x*, we should first determine the measure of the angle that is located at point *O* in the right triangle. To determine this angle, we must calculate what fraction of the circle's area is unshaded. The radius *r* of the circle is 5 and its area is πr^2, or 25π. The area of the shaded region is 20π, so the area of the unshaded region must be 5π. Therefore, the fraction of the circle's area that is unshaded is given by the expression below:

$$5\pi/25\pi = 1/5.$$

A circle contains a total of 360 degrees of arc, which means that 1/5 of 360 degrees, or 72 degrees, is the measure of the angle at point *O* in the unshaded region. Since we now know that two of the three angles in the triangle measure 72 degrees and 90 degrees, and that the sum of the measures of the three angles is always 180 degrees, the third angle must measure 18 degrees. Therefore, *x* = 18.

An object in a circle

The circle in Figure 5.6 (a) has its center at *C*. Given segments of the following lengths 6, 7.0, 7.5, 8.10, and 12, which is the length of the longest line segment that can be placed entirely inside the circle?

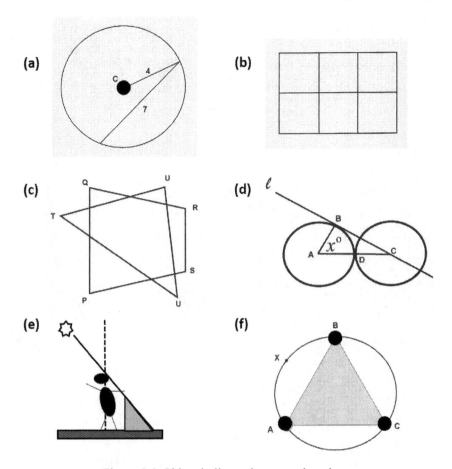

Figure 5.6. Object in lines, shapes, and angles

Solution Logic

Since the radius of the circle is 4, the diameter of the circle is 8. In a circle, the diameter is longer than any segment that can be placed entirely inside the circle. Therefore, segments of length 8.10 or length 14.00 could not be placed entirely within the circle, and the correct answer is 7.5.

61

Practice Squares

In Figure 5.6 (b), the large rectangle is divided into six identical small squares. If the perimeter of the large rectangle is 30, what is the perimeter of one of the small squares?

Solution

The perimeter of one of the small squares can be found if we know the magnitude of its sides. Let each side of the small square be represented by x. Then the perimeter of the large rectangle is calculated as:

$3x + 3x + 2x + 2x = 10x$, which we know is equal to 30.

Therefore, solving for x yields x = 3. Consequently, the perimeter of one of the small squares is $4 \times 3 = 12$.

Sharp Turn Angles

The angle of a turn during a skateboarding run can have a serious and direct implication on how the routine plays out. Sharp turns versus obtuse turns can be practiced so well that the skateboard is kept in strategic motion paths. In Figure 5.6 (c), if *PQRS* is a quadrilateral and *TUV* is a triangle, what is the sum of the degree measures of the marked angles? This can be used to map out how a skateboarder moves from one point to the other at the skateboard park.

In the figure, if *PQRS* is a quadrilateral and *TUV* is a triangle, what is the sum of the degree measures of the marked angles?

A. 420

B. 490

C. 540

D. 560

E. 580

Answer: C

The marked angles in the figure are angles P, Q, R, and S, which are the angles of a quadrilateral, and angles T, U, and V, which are the angles of a triangle. The sum of the degree measures of the angles of a quadrilateral is 360, and the sum of the degree measures of the angles of a triangle is 180. Therefore, the sum of the degree measures of the marked angles is 360 plus 180, which is 540.

Tangent Circle Formations

In Figure 5.6 (d), the circle with center A and the circle with center C are tangent at point D. If the circles each have radius 10, and if line is tangent to the circle with center A at point B, what is the value of x?

A. 55

B. 60

C. 63

D. 65

E. It cannot be determined from the information given.

Answer: B

The circles each have radius 10, so $AB = AD = DC = 10$. Since the circles are tangent at point D, segment contains D and $AC =$

20. Also, and are perpendicular because a line tangent to a circle forms a right angle with the radius at the point of tangency. Therefore, *ABC* is a right triangle with hypotenuse 20 and side of length 10. A right triangle with one side of length one-half that of its hypotenuse is a 30° – 60° – 90° triangle. The 30° angle is opposite side, so $x = 90 - 30 = 60$.

Height and Shadow

Suppose a skateboarder, TJ, is 180 centimeters tall. At 2 PM one day, his shadow is 60 centimeters long, and the shadow of a nearby vertical pole is t centimeters long. In terms of t, what is the height, in centimeters, of the pole?

A. $t + 120$
B. $2t$
C. $3t$
D. $60-t$
E. $60+t$

Answer: C

The problem is pictured in Figure 5.6 (e), where x is the height, in centimeters, of the flag post. There are two right triangles in the figure. One triangle is formed by part of the line from the sun to point P, the perpendicular from TJ's head to the ground, and TJ's shadow along the ground. The other triangle is formed by part of the line from the sun to point P, the perpendicular from the top of the flag post to the ground, and the flag post's shadow along the ground. Since these two right triangles share the acute angle at P, they are similar triangles. Since the corresponding sides of similar triangles are in proportion, it follows that $180/x$

= 60/*t*. Solving this equation for *x*, the height, in centimeters, of the flag post, yields *x* = 3*t*.

Inscribed Triangle

In Figure 5.6 (f), inscribed triangle *ABC* is equilateral. If the radius of the circle is *r*, then the length of arc *AXB* is what?

A. $2\pi r/3$
B. $4\pi r/3$
C. $3\pi r/2$
D. $\pi r^2/3$
E. $2\pi r^2/3$

Answer: A

An equilateral triangle has three equal sides, so the lengths of the three arcs must be equal, and thus, each arc is 1/3 of the circumference of the circle. The circumference of the circle is $2\pi r$, so the length of arc *AXB* is 1/3 of $2\pi r$, or $2\pi r/3$.

Advanced Computations

In composite systems, such as mass-spring systems or skaterboard systems, with negligible friction and damping, we can sometimes use the principle of the conservation of energy to obtain the equation of motion. For simple harmonic motion, we can determine the frequency of vibration without obtaining the equation of motion. Although vibration is not typically an issue in skateboarding, except in some esoteric tricks, the following advanced computations may still be of mathematical and motivational interest.

Problem: In an equation of motion of a mass-spring system, use the energy method to derive the equation of motion of the mass (m) attached to a spring (with stiffness constant, k) and moving in the vertical direction, displacement x. Spring extension is δ_{st} and Spring length is L.

Solution: With the displacement x measured from the equilibrium position, and taking the gravitational potential energy to be zero at $x = 0$, the total potential energy of the system is

$$V = V_s + V_\delta = \frac{1}{2}k\left(x + \delta_{st}\right)^2 - mgx = \frac{1}{2}ks^2 + k\delta_{st}x + \frac{1}{2}k\delta_{st}^2 - mgx$$

Because $k\delta_{st} = mg$ the expression for V becomes

$$V = \frac{1}{2}kx^2 + \frac{1}{2}k\delta_{st}^2$$

The total energy of the system is

$$T + V = \frac{1}{2}mx^2 + \frac{1}{2}kx^2 + \frac{1}{2}k\delta_{st}^2$$

From conservation of mechanical energy, $T + V$ is constant and thus its time derivative is zero. Therefore,

$$\frac{d}{dt}(T + V) = \frac{d}{dt}\left(\frac{1}{2}mx^2\right) + \frac{d}{dt}\left(\frac{1}{2}kx^2\right) + \frac{d}{dt}\left(\frac{1}{2}k\delta_{st}^2\right) = 0$$

Evaluating the derivatives gives

$$m\ddot{x} + kx\dot{x} = 0$$

Canceling $\dot{x}$ gives the equation of motion $m\ddot{x} + ks = 0$.

The Rayleigh's method is another approach for the computation. This uses the principle of the conservation of energy to obtain the natural frequency of a mass-spring system if the spring is linear. This approach is useful because it does not require that we first obtain the equation of motion. The method was developed by Lord Rayleigh and was presented in his **Theory of Sound** in 1847. Rayleigh is considered as one of the founders of the study of acoustics and vibration. In a simple harmonic motion, the kinetic energy is maximum and the potential energy is minimum at the equilibrium position, $x = 0$. When the displacement is maximum, the potential energy is maximum, but the kinetic energy is zero. From the conservation of energy, we have the following:

$$T_{max} + V_{min} = T_{min} + V_{max}$$

Thus

$$T_{max} + V_{min} = 0 + V_{max}$$

or

$$T_{max} = V_{max} - V_{min}$$

For example, for a mass-spring system oscillating vertically, $T = m\dot{x}^2 / 2 \; and \; V = k(x + \delta_{st})^2 / 2 - mgx$, we have,

$$T_{max} = \frac{1}{2}m\left(\dot{x}_{max}\right)^2 = V_{max} - V_{min} = \frac{1}{2}k\left(x_{max} + \delta_{st}\right)^2 - mgx_{max} - \frac{1}{2}k\delta_{st}^2$$

Or

$$\frac{1}{2}m\left(\dot{x}_{max}\right)^2 = \frac{1}{2}k\left(x_{max}\right)^2$$

Where we have used the fact that $k\delta_{st} = mg$. In simple harmonic motion $\left|\dot{x}_{max}\right| = \omega_n\left|x_{max}\right|$, and thus,

$$\frac{1}{2}m\left(\omega_n\left|x_{maz}\right|\right)^2 = \frac{1}{2}k\left|x_{max}\right|^2$$

Cancel $\left|x_{max}\right|^2$ and solve for $\Box_n$ to obtain $\omega_n = \sqrt{k/m}$.

Problem: For a cylinder and spring set, apply Rayleigh's principle to determine the natural frequency of the cylinder. The mass moment of inertia about the cylinder's center of mass is I and its mass is, m. Assume the cylinder rolls without slipping, just as a skateboard wheel might roll down a ramp. Radius of the wheel is R. The angle of ramp incline is α. The angular rotation is $\Box$. Spring constant is k and the displacement is x.

Solution: Take $x = 0$ to be the equilibrium position and Δ to be the static deflection. From the geometry of a circle, we know that if the cylinder does not slip, the $R\theta = x$ where θ is the cylinder rotation angle and $\omega = \dot{\theta}$. Take the gravitational potential energy to be zero at the equilibrium position. The elastic potential energy at equilibrium is $k\Delta^2/2$ and the total potential energy is

$$V = \frac{1}{2}k\left(x+\Delta\right)^2 - mgh$$

Where $h = x \sin \alpha$. Because $mg \sin \alpha = k\Delta$ at equilibrium, the expression for V becomes

$$V = \frac{1}{2}k\left(x^2 + 2x\Delta + \Delta^2\right) - mgx \sin \alpha = \frac{1}{2}kx^2 + \frac{1}{2}k\Delta^2$$

Thus $V_{min} = k\Delta^2/2$. The kinetic energy is

$$T = \frac{1}{2}m\dot{x}^2 + \frac{1}{2}I\dot{\theta}^2 = \frac{1}{2}m\dot{x}^2 + \frac{1}{2}I\frac{\dot{x}^2}{R^2} = \frac{1}{2}\left(m + \frac{I}{R^2}\right)\dot{x}^2$$

The above is true because $\dot{\theta} = \dot{x}/R$. Assuming simple harmonic motion occurs, we obtain $x(t) = A \sin\left(\omega_n t + \varphi\right)$ and $\dot{x} = \omega_n A \cos\left(\omega_n t + \varphi\right)$. Thus $x_{max} = A$, $\dot{x}_{max} = \omega_n A$, and

$$T_{max} = \frac{1}{2}\left(m + \frac{I}{R^2}\right)\left(\omega_n A\right)^2$$

$$V_{max} = \frac{1}{2}kA^2 + \frac{1}{2}k\Delta^2$$

From Rayleigh's method, $T_{max} = V_{max} - V_{min}$, and we have

$$\frac{1}{2}\left(m + \frac{I}{R^2}\right)\left(\omega_n A\right)^2 = \frac{1}{2}kA^2 + \frac{1}{2}k\Delta^2 - \frac{1}{2}k\Delta^2 = \frac{1}{2}kA^2$$

This gives

$$\left(m + \frac{I}{R^2}\right)\omega_n^2 k$$

$$\omega_n = \sqrt{\frac{k}{m + I/R^2}}$$

This is the same answer found previously. We have the free-body diagram method versus the energy method. These computational examples are interesting and they may encourage more exploration by those who are mathematically inclined and curious. Of course, skateboarders don't bother themselves with the mathematics, physics, or dynamics of what they do. They just focus on making their repeated on-track practice work to accomplish their tricks. There is nothing wrong in leaving the mathematics to the on-paper analysts.

CHAPTER 6

POPULAR SKATEBOARDING JUMPS

Now that we have presented some basic technical physics related to the movements in skateboarding, we can better appreciate some of the specifics of skateboarding itself. As we have mentioned before, a basic understanding of physics can help a skateboarder have a better appreciation for the intuitive dynamics that are acquired through gut-wrenching practice.

Many of the tricks of skateboarding have some theory of physics as their basis. In particular, those who are just starting out can be helped if they understand the possibilities and impossibilities of certain moves in the geometrical sense. Som of the most popular jumps are:

1. The Hippie Jump
2. The Ollie
3. Frontside 180
4. Pumping On A Half-Pipe

The descriptions presented below for these jumps are based on experiments, reports, and examples posted online for **The Physics of Skateboarding** on the website of *Real World*

Physics Problems, https://www.real-world-physics-problems. com/physics-of-skateboarding.html (accessed on January 18, 2021).

The Hippie Jump

As conveyed in the online postings at the website, https://www. real-world-physics-problems.com/physics-of-skateboarding. html, the hippie jump is one of the very graceful moves in skateboarding. In this jump routing, a skateboarder rides along on a flat horizontal surface at a certain velocity. He then jumps straight up without exerting any horizontal force on the board. This allows him to "sail" through the air at the same horizontal velocity as the board, which is also already moving at the same speed. As a result, the skateboard remains directly below skateboarder, who is able to land on the board, seemingly, effortlessly because both objects are moving at the same speed. Relative speed is the key in this coordinated process.

You can imagine the impact of a relative speed if you are traveling in an airplane moving at a certain high speed and you through an object horizontally forward in the air within the plane in the same direction as the flight direction of the airplane. The object thrown actually travels linearly forward at the velocity with which it is thrown within the airplane. The net velocity of the object is the velocity at which it and the airplane are traveling in consonant plus the incremental velocity to which the object is subjected. That is the essence of executing the hippie jump in skateboarding.

To execute this trick successfully, the skateboarder must thrust himself up vertically by pushing vertically down with his legs.

If he pushes on the board with any incremental horizontal force, the board will propel away from him in the forward or backward direction. After the skateboarder jumps off the board, gravity takes over and he follows a parabolic arc as he sails through the air before landing back on the board.

The physics behind this jump is the equations of projectile motion, in which only the vertical component of velocity changes because gravity only acts in the vertical direction. The horizontal component of velocity of the skateboarder stays the same since there is no force acting on him in the horizontal direction, if we neglect air resistance. The friction force acting on the board as it rolls along (due to contact with the ground) is small and doesn't slow the board down significantly. Consequently, its velocity is about the same as the horizontal velocity of the skateboarder. This allows the skateboarder to settle back onto the board. To make the jump more challenging, the skateboarder can do the jump over an obstacle. Readers are directed to the website of *Real World Physics Problems* to read more about this exciting skateboarding jump and others.

The Ollie

The Ollie is a basic jump trick in skateboarding, upon which other more complicate jumps are attempted. The beginning of the Ollie consists of two basic actions, occurring roughly simultaneously, as summarized below:

1. The skateboarder jumps up and off the board. This is accompanied by him pushing down quickly on the tail end of the board, causing it to rebound off the ground and bounce back up.

2. The skateboarder guides the board along with his feet as it flies through the air, enabling him to land back on top of it. Figure 6.1 illustrates an example of the Ollie.

3.

Figure 6.1. Example of Starting a Hippie Jump
(Courtesy TJ Photos)

The Ollie is typically executed in four segments:

- The skateboarder is crouched down and is preparing to jump off the board. His right foot is on the tail of the board and his left foot is near the middle of the board. The three forces all balance out to zero in this stage since the board is stationary, without acceleration.

- The skater propels himself upward by explosively straightening his legs and lifting up his arms, both for balancing and forming force components. At the same time, he pushes down with his right foot much harder than with his left foot. This causes the board to tilt back and strike the ground with the tail. When the tail strikes the ground a large vertical impulse force is generated with the ground. We remember Newton's Laws of motion here. This propels the board upward and also causes the board to rotate clockwise. The skateboarder then slides his left foot to the left along the board and tilts it somewhat, allowing him to snatch the rough surface of the board using the edge of his shoe. This enables him to guide the board airborne along the remainder of the motion. The force exerted on the board by his left foot is broken down into two components, one perpendicular to the board and the other parallel to the board. The parallel component of this force is what moves the board along.
- In the third segment, the skateboarder's right foot has lost contact with the board. He is guiding the board along with his left foot and dragging the board upward even higher.
- In the fourth segment, the skateboarder brings the board into the horizontal position by pushing down with his left foot, while raising his right foot, in order to get it out of the way of the rising tail of the board. At this point, the skateboarder is making contact with the board with both of his feet and he is now able to land squarely on the board.

With frequent and dedicated practice, the process narrated above is done smoothly and effortlessly, without a conscious reference to the physics and dynamics of the various actions. Figure 6.2 demonstrates skateboarding routine of accomplishing an upward vertical jump by the skateboarder in unison with the skateboard onto an elevated flat surface.

Figure 6.2. Example of Vertical Jump onto an elevated flat surface
(Courtesy TJ Photos)

Frontside 180

The physics of the frontside 180 involves the conservation of angular momentum. In this trick the skateboarder rotates his board 180 degrees in the air so that, upon landing, he is facing in the opposite direction from the initial direction. He does this even though his initial angular momentum is zero, meaning he is not rotating initially. As the skateboarder gets airborne, the only force acting on him is gravity, which acts though the center of mass of the system (consisting of skater plus board). Because of this, the gravity force cannot exert a torque on the skateboarder-and-skateboard system. So, as a whole the composite system cannot rotate.

There is an interesting physics behind executing this rotational trick. The skater managers to rotate the board 180 degrees by the time he lands back on the ground. This is done by rotating his upper body and lower body in opposite directions. This way he can land with the board facing the other way, while still adhering to the physical requirement that the angular momentum of the system remains zero. The skater gives his upper body a clockwise twist, resulting in an angular momentum of the upper body to achieve Level 1. At the same time, he gives his lower body, including the skateboard, a counterclockwise rotation, resulting in an angular momentum for the lower body and skateboard to reach Level 2. Since angular momentum is conserved for the system, Level 1 + Level 2 will cancel out to equate to zero. The key is for the skateboarder to generate a high enough Level 1 angular momentum so that his lower body, including the skateboard, must match this value by a magnitude of Level 2 by rotating 180 degrees in the other direction. The skateboarder does this by extending out his arms while he is airborne. This increases the rotational inertia of the upper body, which increases Level 1. In this routine, the following equation is applicable:

$$\text{Angular momentum} = (I)(w),$$

where I is the rotational inertia and w is the angular velocity of the body. Once the skateboarder lands on the ground, he rotates his upper body back around. He is able to do this after landing because he is able to exert a torque against the ground, allowing him to rotate his body back around so that he is now facing entirely in the opposite direction to before. Again, this might sound complicated in narrative, but it is easily achievable through repeated trials and errors.

Other popular skateboarding tricks include "pumping on a half-pipe," which is used by skateboarders to increase their vertical take-off speed when they exit the pipe (a curved ramp). This enables them to reach greater height and perform more tricks, while airborne. By continually pumping his body through crouching down and lifting his body and arms up in the curved portion of the half-pipe, the skateboarder is able to continually increase his velocity, eventually allowing sufficient height to be reached (upon exiting the half-pipe) to perform a variety of acrobatic mid-air tricks. The pumping and height increases are similar to pumping on a swing with alternating leg extension and contraction, which adds energy, making the swing to go higher and higher. As a skateboarder lifts his arms and body up, there is a resistance due to the force of centripetal acceleration which tends to push his body away from the center of rotation. This resistance confirms that work is being done and energy is being added to the composite system of the skateboarder and the skateboard (as a unit).

There is a lot more mathematical calculations involved in the collection of skateboarding tricks than we intend to provide in this introductory book. The idea is to whet the appetite of readers for the interest in the physics of skateboarding, not to scare them off with mathematical elucidations.

Speed, Velocity, Acceleration, and Quickness

Along with daredevil courage, skateboarding also requires an interplay of speed, velocity, acceleration, and quickness. We have talked about velocity in describing the dynamics of skateboarding. So, what is the difference between speed, velocity, and quickness.

Speed is the time-based rate at which an object is moving along a path at a particular instant. It ascertains how fast a body moves at a particular time. **Velocity** is the rate and direction of a moving object. Put in another way, speed is a scalar quantity (raw real number), which is a physical measure of magnitude. Whereas, velocity ascertains both the object's speed as well as its direction of movement. That is, velocity is a vector quantity. **Acceleration** is the rate of change of velocity per unit of time. Both velocity and acceleration use speed as a starting point in their measurements. In this context, speed is the measurement of distance traveled over a period of time. For example, a skateboarder may start with an initial speed of zero (stationary) and then ramp down quickly, aided by gravity, to a high rate of speed, based on the acceleration facilitated by gravity. What the skateboarder does (in his tricks) is a function of **quickness**, which is his ability to react quickly to the dynamics around him. Anecdotally speaking, quickness is the ability of the skateboarder to react and outmaneuver impediments in his path. The most successful skateboarders are those who can master the interplay of courage, speed, velocity, acceleration, and quickness to increase the accuracy of the intended skateboarding tricks.

Practice makes Perfect. Good luck!

Chapter 6 Reference

Real World Physics Problems (2021), The Physics of Skateboarding, https://www.real-world-physics-problems.com/physics-of-skateboarding.html, accessed January 17, 2021

CHAPTER 7

BALANCING SPORTS, RECREATION, AND EDUCATION

As mentioned earlier, one primary goal of this book is to get readers excited about the power and utility of science and mathematics in sports. If the contents of this book can be leveraged to spark an interest in further STEM education, then our purpose will have been served.

This chapter presents a brief introduction to each of the elements of STEM. Although the primary audience for the book is adolescents, younger kids can also benefit from the early introduction to the principles of STEM. Studies have shown that children under the age of 6 are capable of learning multiple languages. As early as possible, the brain gets wired for multiple lanes of language reasoning. So, why not get them to start learning the language of STEM earlier on? In other words, children can learn to "speak" math and science very early as they embark upon a lifetime of education. Coupling the learning experience with the fun of sports participation makes the overall process much more effective. It is in this regard that we advocate balancing Sports, Recreation, and Education as illustrated in Figure 7.1. With our world becoming more and more digitally driven, the workforce of the future will be more of knowledge workers rather than the traditional shop-floor labor. Education is the pathway for acquiring the new knowledge that will be required to function and contribute to that emerging society. In this regard, it is essential to embrace and leverage all educational opportunities available to youths. Meanwhile, sports are essential for building character and teamwork. Recreation provides a relaxing avocation from the hustle and bustle of a fast-paced digital society. In all these, the key to a rewarding life is to learn to balance all the pursuits. As the adage goes, all work and no play makes an individual a dull person. Similarly, all play and no work or recreational break can break the spirit of a person. Because the premise of this book is on physics, this chapter presents a brief description of the elements of STEM (Science, Technology, Engineering, and Mathematics) in the context of general educational awareness.

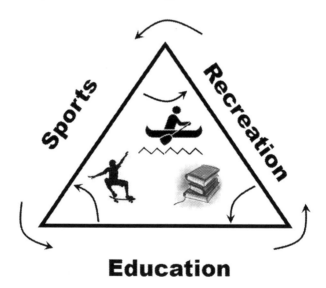

Figure 7.1. Balancing sports, education, and recreation

Science

Science (from the Latin word, *scientia*, meaning "knowledge") refers to any systematic knowledge or practice. In its more usual interpretation, science refers to a system of acquiring knowledge based on scientific method, as well as to the organized body of knowledge gained through such research. Science consists of two major categories:

- Experimental science
- Applied science

Experimental science is based on experiments (Latin: *ex-periri*, "to try out") as a method of investigating causal relationships among variables and factors. Applied science is the application of scientific research to specific human needs. Experimental science and applied science are often interconnected.

Science is the effort to discover and increase human understanding of how the real world works. Its focus is on reality that is independent of religious, political, cultural, or philosophical preferences.

Using controlled methods, scientists collect data in the form of observations, record observable physical evidence of natural phenomena, and analyze the information to construct theoretical explanations of how things work.

Knowledge in science is gained through research. The methods of scientific research include the generation of conjectures (hypotheses) about how something works. Experimentations are conducted to test these hypotheses under controlled conditions. The outcome of this empirical scientific process is the formulation of theory that describes human understanding of physical processes and facilitates prediction of what to expect in certain situations.

A broader and more modern definition of science includes the natural sciences along with the *social* and *behavioral sciences,* as the main subdivisions. This involves the observation, identification, description, experimental investigation, and theoretical explanation of phenomenon. The social and behavioral aspects of skateboarding buddies make the sport particularly amenable to the application of science in its broad sense.

Technology

A strict definition of technology is quite elusive. But in its basic form, it relates to how humans develop and use tools. Knowledge and usage of tools and crafts constitute the application of knowledge. Technology is a term with origins in the Greek word *technologia,* formed from *techne,* ("craft") and *logia,* ("saying"). Technology can refer to material objects of use by the society, such as machines, hardware or utensils. It can also encompass broad areas covering systems, methods of organization, and techniques. The term can be applied generally or to specific areas of application, including:

- Communication technology (e.g., cell phones)
- Construction technology (e.g., super highways)
- Medical technology (e.g., x-ray imaging)
- Weapons technology (e.g., guns)

The origin of humans' use of technology dates back to the conversion of natural resources into simple tools (e.g., stones to arrow heads). The pre-historical discovery of the ability to control fire increased the available sources of food. The invention of the wheel helped humans in traveling long distances from home base. The development of the roof enabled humans to control their environment and place of abode. Recent technological advances, including computers, wireless interfaces, and the Internet, have minimized physical barriers to communication and allowed humans to interact on a global scale. The capability of technology often advances on a geometric scale. For example, we have war-fighting technology moving from pre-historic weapon of clubs to the modern weapon of nuclear bombs.

Technology has facilitated more advanced economies that benefit the entire society, such as the emerging global economy. Technology has made it possible for us to participate in more leisure time and assume better working conditions.

Engineering

Engineering is the body of knowledge related the science of building or constructing something. It is the discipline and profession of applying technical, scientific and mathematical knowledge in order to utilize natural laws and physical resources to help design and implement materials, structures, machines, devices, systems, and processes that safely realize a desired objective.

The discipline dates back to thousands of years and it has shaped the origin of modern human development as we know it today. Engineering has been practiced since pre-historic times.

The common characteristics of engineers through the centuries have been an interest in exploratory engagements and intellectual curiosity about how to build things, both physical and conceptual. Common engineering inquiries include:

- What
- Who
- Where
- Why
- When
- How

These inquiries are sometimes represented by the following mnemonic equation:

$$E = W^5H$$

Because of its wide applications, engineering is very diverse and ubiquitous in human endeavors. The major branches of engineering offer a variety of career fields and options, including the following:

- Aerospace engineering
- Astronautical engineering
- Agricultural engineering
- Architectural engineering
- Bio-medical engineering
- Ceramic engineering
- Chemical engineering
- Civil engineering
- Electrical engineering
- Geological engineering
- Industrial engineering

- Marine engineering
- Materials engineering
- Mechanical engineering
- Metallurgical engineering
- Mining engineering
- Nuclear engineering
- Petroleum engineering

Mathematics

Mathematics is the foundation for applying science, technology, and engineering to solve problems. It is the study of quantity, structure, space, change, and related topics of pattern and form.

Mathematicians seek out patterns whether found in numbers, space, natural science, computers, imaginary abstractions, or elsewhere. Mathematicians formulate new conjectures and establish their truth by precise deduction from axioms and definitions that are chosen based on the prevailing problem scenario.

The most common branches of mathematics for everyday application are:

- Algebra
- Calculus
- Geometry
- Trigonometry
- Differential equations

Algebra is the mathematics of quantities (known and unknown). Calculus is the mathematics of variations (i.e., changes in variables). Geometry is the mathematics of size, shape, and relative position of figures and with properties of space. Trigonometry is the mathematics of triangles and their angles (interior and exterior). It is the study of how the sides and angles of a triangle interrelate to one another. A differential equation is a mathematical equation for an unknown function of one or several variables that relates the values of the function itself and its derivatives of various orders. Differential equations play a prominent role in engineering, physics, economics and other disciplines.

Summary

This book has presented some basic principles of physics as applied to the sport of skateboarding. The presentations and discussions are selected to illustrate the complexities involved in analysis the dynamics of skateboarding without dousing the interest of those who are not mathematically inclined. We hope every reader will gain something from the book whether for a fun and leisurely reading or for a serious introductory exposition that can lead to further studies. On this note, we hope we have gotten many readers excited about the fun and joy of physics in sports in general, not just in skateboarding.

APPENDIX

CONVERSION FACTORS

Units of Measurement	
English system	
1 foot (ft)	12 inches (in)
1 yard (yd)	3 feet
1 mile (mi)	1760 yards
1 sq. foot	144 sq. inches
1 sq. yard	9 sq. feet
1 acre	4840 sq. yards

Metric system		
mm	millimeter	.001 m
cm	centimeter	.01 m
dm	decimeter	.1 m
m	meter	1 m
dam	decameter	10 m
hm	hectometer	100 m
km	kilometer	1000 m

CONSTANTS	
speed of light	$2.997,925 \times 10^{10}$ cm/sec 983.6×10^{6} ft/sec 186,284 miles/sec
velocity of sound	340.3 meters/sec 1116 ft/sec
Gravity (acceleration)	9.80665 m/sec square 32.174 ft/sec square 386.089 inches/sec square

AREA CONVERSION		
Multiply	**by**	**to Obtain**
acres	43,560	sq feet
acres	4,047	sq meters
acres	4,840	sq yards
acres	0.405	hectare
sq cm	0.155	sq inches
sq feet	144	sq inches
sq feet	0.09290	sq meters
sq feet	0.1111	sq yards
sq inches	645.16	sq millimeters
sq kilometers	0.3861	sq miles
sq meters	10.764	sq feet
sq meters	1.196	sq yards
sq miles	640	acres
sq miles	2.590	sq kilometers

VOLUME CONVERSION		
Multiply	**by**	**to Obtain**
acre-foot	1233.5	cubic meters
cubic cm	0.06102	cubic inches
cubic feet	1728	cubic inches
	7.480	gallons (US)
	0.02832	cubic meters
	0.03704	cubic yards
liter	1.057	liquid quarts
	0.908	dry quarts
	61.024	Cubic inches
Gallons (US)	231	cubic inches
	3.7854	liters
	4	quarts
	0.833	British gallons
	128	U.S. fluid ounces
quarts (US)	0.9463	liters

ENERGY, HEAT, AND POWER CONVERSION		
Multiply	**by**	**to Obtain**
BTU	1055.9	joules
BTU	0.2520	kg-calories
watt-hour	3600	joules
watt-hour	3.409	BTU
HP (electric)	746	watts
BTU/second	1055.9	watts
Watt-second	1.00	joules

MASS CONVERSION		
Multiply	**by**	**to Obtain**
carat	0.200	cubic grams
grams	0.03527	ounces
kilograms	2.2046	pounds
ounces	28.350	grams
pound	16	ounces
pound	453.6	grams
stone (UK)	6.35	kilograms
stone (UK)	14	pounds
ton (net)	907.2	kilograms
ton (net)	2000	pounds
ton (net)	0.893	gross ton
ton (net)	0.907	metric ton
ton (gross)	ton (gross)	pounds
ton (gross)	1.12	net tons
ton (gross)	1.016	metric tons
tonne (metric)	2,204.623	pounds
tonne (metric)	0.984	gross pound
tonne (metric)	1000	kilograms

TEMPERATURE CONVERSION	
Celsius to Kelvin	$K = C + 273.15$
Celsius to Fahrenheit	$F = (9/5)C + 32$
Fahrenheit to Celsius	$C = (5/9)(F - 32)$
Fahrenheit to Kelvin	$K = (5/9)(F + 459.67)$
Fahrenheit to Rankin	$R = F + 459.67$
Rankin to Kelvin	$K = (5/9)R$

VELOCITY CONVERSION		
Multiply	**by**	**to Obtain**
feet/minute	5.080	mm/second
feet/second	0.3048	meters/second
inches/second	0.0254	meters/second
km/hour	0.6214	miles/hour
meters/second	3.2808	feet/second
meters/second	2.237	miles/hour
miles/hour	88.0	feet/minute
miles/hour	0.44704	meters/second
miles/hour	1.6093	km/hour
miles/hour	0.8684	knots
knot	1.151	miles/hour

PRESSURE CONVERSION		
Multiply	**by**	**to Obtain**
atmospheres	1.01325	bars
	33.90	feet of water
	29.92	inches of mercury
	760.0	mm of mercury
bars	75.01	cm of mercury
	14.50	pounds/sq inch
dyne/sq cm	0.1	N/sq meter
newtons/sq cm	1.450	pounds/sq inch
pounds/sq inch	0.06805	atmospheres
	2.036	inches of mercury
	27.708	inches of water
	68.948	millibars
	51.72	mm of mercury

DISTANCE CONVERSION		
Multiply	**by**	**to Obtain**
angstrom	10^{-10}	meters
feet	0.30480	meters
feet	12	meters
inches	25.40	millimeters
inches	0.02540	meters
inches	0.08333	feet
kilometers	3,280.8	feet
kilometers	0.6214	miles
kilometers	1,094	yards
meters	39.370	inches
meters	3.2808	feet
meters	1.094	yards
miles	5,280	feet
miles	1.6093	kilometers
miles	0.8694	nautical miles
millimeters	0.03937	inches
nautical miles	6,076	feet
nautical miles	1.852	kilometers
yards	0.9144	meters
yards	3	feet
yards	36	inches

HOUSEHOLD MEASUREMENTS

1 pinch ....1/8 teaspoon or less

3 teaspoons ....1 tablespoon

2 tablespoons ....1/8 cup

4 tablespoons ....1/4 cup

8 tablespoons ....1/2 cup

12 tablespoons ....3/4 cup

16 tablespoons ....1 cup

5 tablespoons + 1 teaspoon ....1/3 cup

4 oz ....1/2 cup

8oz ....1 cup

16 oz ....1 lb

1 oz ....2 tablespoons fat or liquid

1 cup of liquid ....1/2 pint

2 cups ....1 pint

2 pints ....1 quart

4 cup of liquid ....1 quart

4 quarts ....1 gallon

8 quarts ....1 peck (such as apples, pears, etc.)

1 jigger ....1 ½ fluid oz

1 jigger ....3 tablespoons

NUMBERS, PREFIXES, AND POWER	
Notation	**Expansion**
quecca (10^{30})	1, 000, 000, 000, 000, 000, 000, 000, 000, 000, 000, 000, 000
ronna (10^{27})	1, 000, 000, 000, 000, 000, 000, 000, 000, 000
yotta (10^{24})	1, 000, 000, 000, 000, 000, 000, 000, 000
zetta (10^{21})	1, 000, 000, 000, 00,0 000, 000, 000
exa (10^{18})	1, 000, 000, 000, 000, 000, 000
peta (10^{15})	1, 000, 000, 000, 000, 000
tera (10^{12})	1, 000, 000, 000, 000
giga (10^{9})	1, 000, 000, 000
mega (10^{6})	1, 000, 000
kilo (10^{3})	1, 000
hecto (10^{2})	100
deca (10^{1})	10
deci (10^{-1})	0.1
centi (10^{-2})	0.01
milli (10^{-3})	0.001
micro (10^{-6})	0.000 001
nano (10^{-9})	0.000 000 001
pico (10^{-12})	0.000 000 000 001
femto (10^{-15})	0.000 000 000 000 001
atto (10^{-18})	0.000 000 000 000 000 001
zepto (10^{-21})	0.000 000 000 000 000 000 001
yocto (10^{-24})	0.000 000 000 000 000 000 000 001
ronto (10^{-27})	0.000 000 000 000 000 000 000 000 001
quecto (10^{-30})	0.000 000 000 000 000 000 000 000 000 001
stringo (10^{-35})	0.000 000 000 000 000 000 000 000 000 000 000 01

Trigonometric Relationships

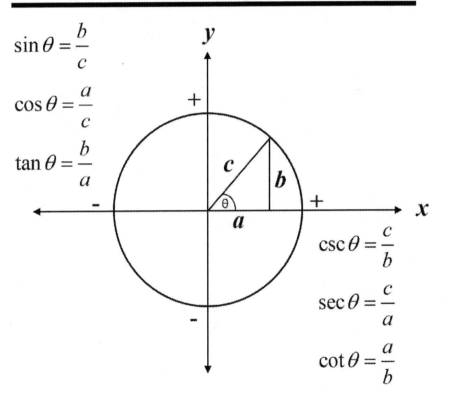

$$\sin\theta = \frac{b}{c}$$

$$\cos\theta = \frac{a}{c}$$

$$\tan\theta = \frac{b}{a}$$

$$\csc\theta = \frac{c}{b}$$

$$\sec\theta = \frac{c}{a}$$

$$\cot\theta = \frac{a}{b}$$

Printed in the United States
By Bookmasters